INTRODUCTION

Welcome back to FastTrack®!

Hope you enjoyed Keyboard 1 and are ready to play some hits. Have you and your friends formed a band? Or do you feel like soloing with the audio tracks? Either way, make sure you're turned up loud... it's time to jam!

The eight songs in this book appear in the order of their difficulty. With the knowledge you already have, you're ready to play all of these songs. But it's still important to remember the three Ps: **patience**, **practice** and **pace yourself**.

As with Keyboard 1, don't try to bite off more than you can chew. If your hands hurt, take some time off. If you get frustrated, relax and just listen to the tracks. If you forget a chord or note position, go back and learn it. If you're doing fine, think about charging admission.

CONTENTS

ABOUT THE AUDIO

Again, you get audio tracks with the book! Each song in the book is included, so you can hear how it sounds and play along when you're ready.

Each audio example is preceded by one measure of "clicks" to indicate the tempo and meter. Pan right to hear the keyboard part emphasized. Pan left to hear the accompaniment emphasized.

To access audio visit:
www.halleonard.com/mylibrary

7096-1766-9742-0975

ISBN 978-0-7935-7414-8

HAL•LEONARD®
CORPORATION
7777 W. BLUEMOUND RD. P.O. BOX 13819 MILWAUKEE, WI 53213

Visit Hal Leonard Online at
www.halleonard.com

LEARN SOMETHING NEW EACH DAY

We know you're eager to play, but first you need to learn a few new things. We'll make it brief—only two pages...

Melody and Lyrics

All of the melody lines and lyrics to these great songs are included for your musical pleasure (and benefit). These are shown on an extra musical staff, which we added above your part.

Sometimes you will be playing this melody, too. Other times you're supporting this melody with chords. Either way, you can easily follow the song as you play your part.

And whether you have a singer in the band or decide to carry the tune yourself, this new staff is your key to adding some vocals to your tunes.

New Chords

In addition to the many chords you learned in *Keyboard 1*, three of the songs contain some new chords. Here they are in diagrams. They're easy but require practice.

"Oh, Pretty Woman"

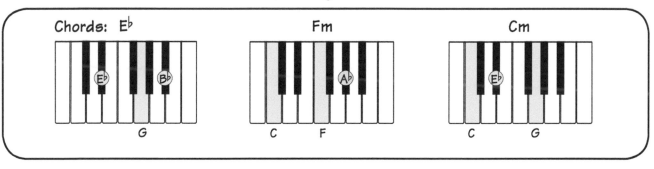

"Your Song"

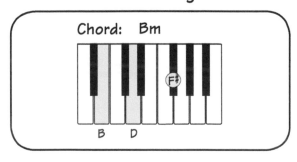

Play 'em a few times to get the feel...

Endings

Several of the songs have some interesting little symbols that you must understand before playing. Each of these symbols represents a different type of ending.

1st and 2nd Endings

You know these from *Keyboard 1* (the brackets with numbers):

REMINDER: Simply play the song through to the first ending, repeat back to the first repeat sign, or beginning of the song (whichever is the case). Play through the song again, but skip the first ending and play the second ending.

D.S. al Coda

When you see these words, go back and repeat from this symbol: 𝄋

Play until you see the words *"To Coda"* then skip to the Coda, indicated by this symbol: 𝄌

Now just finish the song.

Song Structure

Most songs have different sections, which might be recognizable by any or all of the following:

 INTRODUCTION (or "intro"): This is a short section at the beginning that (you guessed it again!) "introduces" the song to the listeners.

 VERSES: One of the main sections of the song is the **verse**. There will usually be several verses, all with the same music but each with different lyrics.

 CHORUS: Another main section of a song is the **chorus**. Again, there might be several choruses, but each chorus will often have the same lyrics and music.

 BRIDGE: This section makes a transition from one part of a song to the next. For example, you may find a **bridge** between the chorus and next verse.

 SOLOS: Sometimes **solos** are played over the verse or chorus structure, but in some songs the solo section has its own structure. This is your time to shine!

 OUTRO: Similar to the "intro," this section brings the song to an end.

That's about it! Enjoy the music...

❶ You Really Got Me

Words and Music by Ray Davies

5

Wild Thing

Words and Music by Chip Taylor

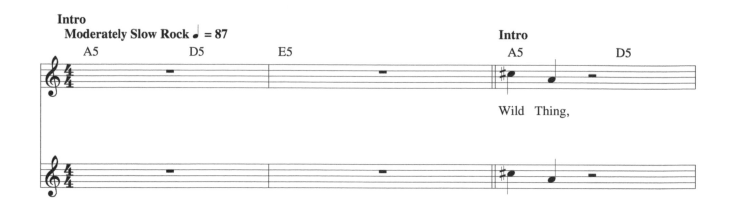

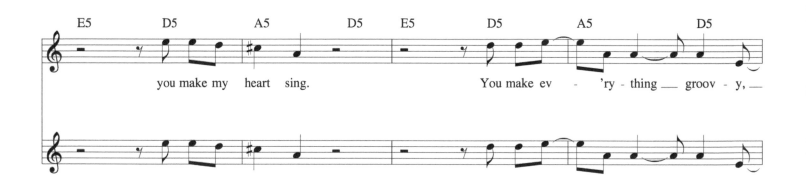

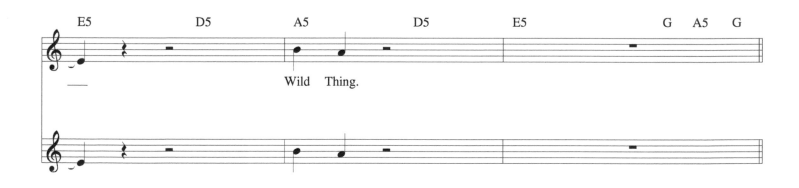

* 2nd time only.

◆3 I Want to Hold Your Hand

Words and Music by John Lennon and Paul McCartney

4 Wonderful Tonight

Words and Music by Eric Clapton

Intro
Moderately Slow ♩ = 95

1. It's late in the eve - 'ning. _____ She's wond'ring what clothes ____
2. We go to a par - ty, _____ and ev - 'ry - one turns ____
3. It's time to go home ____ now. _____ I've got an ach - ing

to wear. ___ She puts on her make - up ___
to see ___ this beau-ti-ful la - dy ___
head. I give her the car ___ keys, ___

and brush-es her long ___ blond hair. ___ And then she asks ___
is walk-in' a - round ___ with me. ___ And then she asks ___
and she helps me to bed. And then I tell ___

___ me, ___ "Do I look al - right?" ___ And I say,
___ me, ___ "Do ya feel al - right?" ___ And I say,
___ her, ___ as I turn out the light, ___ I say, "My

1.

To Coda ⊕

C   D   G

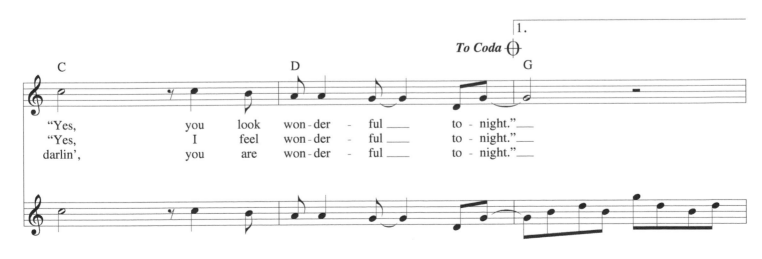

"Yes, you look won-der - ful ___ to - night." ___
"Yes, I feel won-der - ful ___ to - night." ___
darlin', you are won-der - ful ___ to - night." ___

Your Song

Words and Music by Elton John and Bernie Taupin

mon-ey, _____ but, boy, if ___ I did, _____ I'd buy ___ a big

1.

house where ___ we both ___ could live.

2.

live.

Chorus

And you ___ can tell

ev - 'ry- bod - y this ___ is your song. ___ It may ___ be

quite ____ sim - ple, but now that it's done, _____

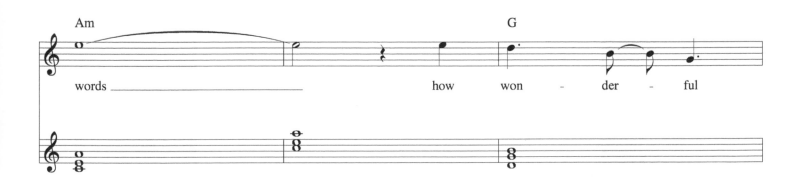

words _____ how won - der - ful

Outro

life is __ while you're _ in __ the world.

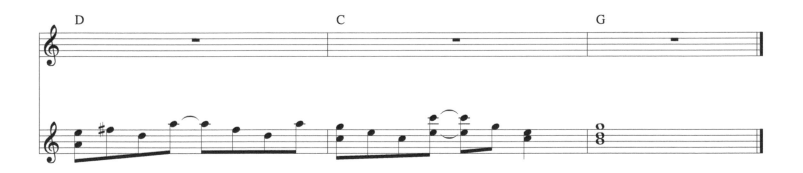

Additional Lyrics

2. If I was a sculptor, but then again no
   or a man who makes potions in a travelin' show…
   I know it's not much, but it's the best I can do.
   My gift is my song and this one's for you.

3. I sat on the roof and kicked off the moss.
   Well, a few of the verses well, they've got me quite cross.
   But the sun's been quite kind while I wrote this song.
   It's for people like you that keep it turned on.

4. So excuse me forgetting, but these things I do.
   You see I've forgotten if they're green, ha, or they're blue.
   Anyway, the thing is, what I really mean,
   Yours are the sweetest eyes I've ever seen.

6 Oh, Pretty Woman

Words and Music by Roy Orbison and Bill Dees

lieve you. _____ It must be true.   No one could look   as   good   as
love - ly _____ as you can be.   Are you lone - ly   just   like

N.C.

you.
me?

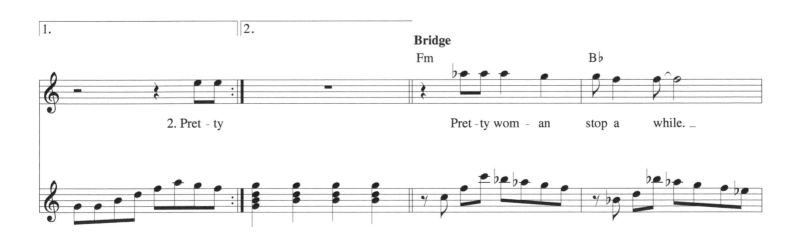

|1. |2.

Bridge
Fm   B♭

2. Pret - ty   Pret -ty wom - an   stop a   while. _

E♭   Cm   Fm   B♭

Pret -ty wom - an,   talk a   while. _   Pret -ty wom - an,   give your   smile _   to

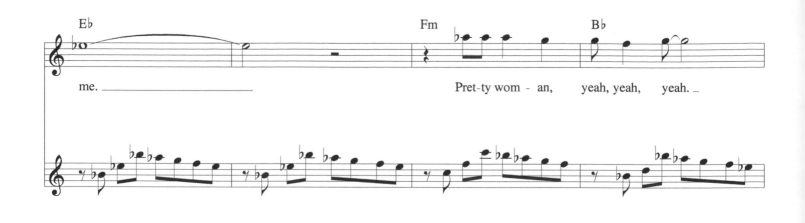

me. _____ Pret-ty wom - an, yeah, yeah, yeah. _

Pret-ty wom - an look my way. _ Pret-ty wom - an, say you'll stay _ with

me, _____ 'cause I need you, _ need you to -

night. Come with me, ba - by. _ Be mine to -

night. _____ 3. Pret-ty

⊕ *Coda*

walk a - way, _____ hey. _____ O. __

__ K.   If that's the way it must be   O. __ K.

I guess I'll   go   on   home. _ It's late. __   There'll be   to -

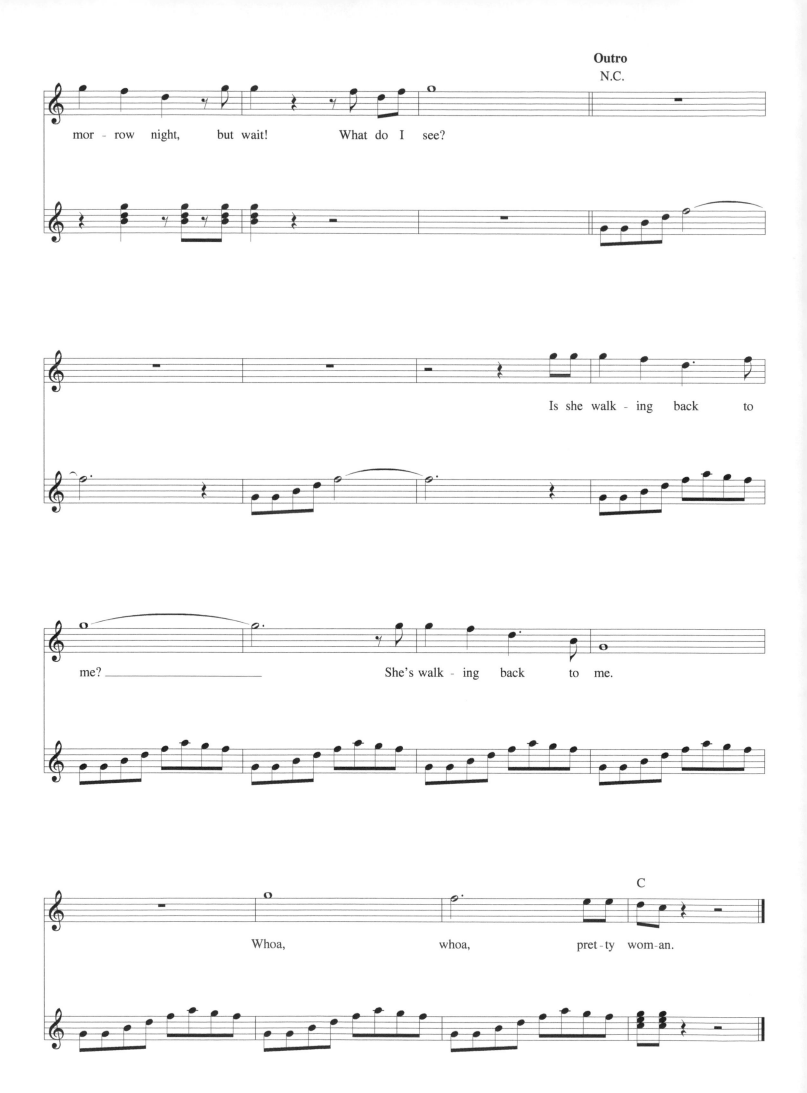

Brown Eyed Girl

Words and Music by Van Morrison

1. Hey where did we ___ go?
2., 3. *See Additional Lyrics*

Days ___ when the rains ___

___ came,

down ___ in the hol-low

play-in' a new ___

___ game,

laugh-ing and a - run-ning, hey, ___ hey,

skip-ping and a -

jump-ing.   In the mist - y morn - ing fog __ with   our

hearts a-thump - in', and   you,   my Brown Eyed Girl. _____

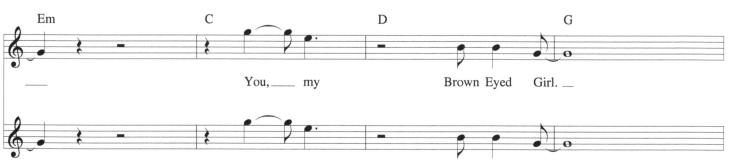

— You, __ my   Brown Eyed   Girl. __

1.   2.

To Coda

Do you re-mem - ber when   we used to sing;_

Chorus

— sha la, __ la, __ la, __ la, la, __ la, __ la, __ la, __ la, la, te da. __

Sha la, __ la, la, __ la, la, __ la, la, __ la, la la, te da. __ La te da.

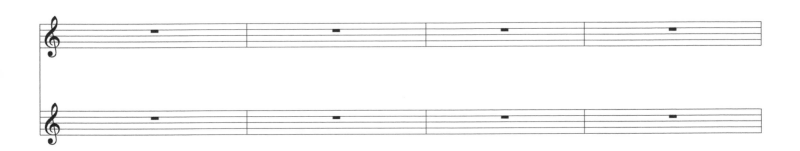

D.S. al Coda
(take 2nd ending)

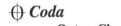 ⊕ *Coda*
Outro–Chorus

Repeat and Fade

__ sha la, __ la, la, __ la, la, __ la, la, __ la, la la, te da. __

Additional Lyrics

2. Whatever happened to Tuesday and so slow
   Going down the old mine with a transistor radio
   Standing in the sunlight laughing
   Hiding behind a rainbow's wall
   Slipping and a–sliding
   All along the waterfall
   With you, my Brown Eyed Girl.
   You, my Brown Eyed Girl.
   Do you remember when we used to sing:
   Chorus

3. So hard to find my way, now that I'm all on my own
   I saw you just the other day, my, how you have grown
   Cast my memory back there, Lord
   Sometime I'm overcome thinking 'bout
   Making love in the green grass
   Behind the stadium
   With you, my Brown Eyed Girl
   With you, my Brown Eyed Girl.
   Do you remember when we used to sing:
   Chorus

Great Balls of Fire

Words and Music by Otis Blackwell and Jack Hammer

FastTrack is the fastest way for beginners to learn to play the instrument they just bought. FastTrack is different from other method books: we've made our book/audio packs user-friendly with plenty of cool songs that make it easy and fun for players to teach themselves. Plus, the last section of the books have the same songs so that students can form a band and jam together. Songbooks for guitar, bass, keyboard and drums are all compatible, and feature eight songs. All packs include great play-along audio with a professional-sounding back-up band.

FastTrack Bass
by Blake Neely & Jeff Schroedl

Level 1
00264732 Method Book/Online Media $14.99
00697284 Method Book/Online Audio $7.99
00696404 Method Book/Online Audio + DVD ... $14.99
00697289 Songbook 1/Online Audio $12.99
00695368 Songbook 2/Online Audio $12.99
00696440 Rock Songbook with CD $12.99
00696058 DVD $7.99

Level 2
00697294 Method Book/Online Audio $9.99
00697298 Songbook 1/Online Audio $12.99
00695369 Songbook 2/Online Audio $12.99

FastTrack Drum
by Blake Neely & Rick Mattingly

Level 1
00264733 Method Book/Online Media $14.99
00697285 Method Book/Online Audio $7.99
00696405 Method Book/Online Audio + DVD ... $14.99
00697290 Songbook 1/Online Audio $12.99
00695367 Songbook 2/Online Audio $12.99
00696441 Rock Songbook with CD $12.99
00696059 DVD $7.99

Level 2
00697295 Method Book/Online Audio $9.99
00697299 Songbook 1/Online Audio $12.99
00695371 Songbook 2/Online Audio $12.99

FastTrack Guitar
For Electric or Acoustic Guitar, or Both
by Blake Neely & Jeff Schroedl

Level 1
00264731 Method Book/Online Media $14.99
00697282 Method Book/Online Audio $7.99
00696403 Method Book/Online Audio + DVD ... $14.99
00697287 Songbook 1/Online Audio $12.99
00695343 Songbook 2/Online Audio $12.99
00696438 Rock Songbook with CD $12.99
00696057 DVD $7.99

Level 2
00697286 Method Book/Online Audio $9.99
00697296 Songbook/Online Audio $14.99

Chords & Scales
00697291 Book/Online Audio $10.99

FastTrack Keyboard
For Electric Keyboard, Synthesizer or Piano
by Blake Neely & Gary Meisner

Level 1
00264734 Method Book/Online Media $14.99
00697283 Method Book/Online Audio $7.99
00696406 Method Book/Online Audio + DVD ... $14.99
00697288 Songbook 1/Online Audio $12.99
00696439 Rock Songbook with CD $12.99
00696060 DVD $7.99

Level 2
00697293 Method Book/Online Audio $9.99

Chords & Scales
00697292   Book/Online Audio $9.99

FastTrack Harmonica
by Blake Neely & Doug Downing

Level 1
00695407 Method Book/Online Audio $7.99
00695958 Mini Method Book with CD $7.95
00820016 Mini Method/CD + Harmonica $12.99
00695574 Songbook/Online Audio $12.99

Level 2
00695889 Method Book/Online Audio $9.99
00695891 Songbook with CD $12.99

FastTrack Lead Singer
by Blake Neely

Level 1
00695408 Method Book/Online Audio $7.99
00695410 Songbook/Online Audio $14.99

Level 2
00695890 Method Book/Online Audio $9.95
00695892 Songbook with CD $12.95

FastTrack Saxophone
by Blake Neely

Level 1
00695241 Method Book/Online Audio $7.99
00695409 Songbook/Online Audio $14.99

FastTrack Ukulele
by Chad Johnson

Level 1
00114417 Method Book/Online Audio $7.99
00158671 Songbook/Online Audio $12.99

Level 2
00275508 Method Book/Online Audio $9.99

FastTrack Violin
by Patrick Clark

Level 1
00141262 Method Book/Online Audio $7.99

HAL•LEONARD®
Visit Hal Leonard online at www.halleonard.com

*Prices, contents, and availability subject to change without notice.
Some products may not be available outside the U.S.A. Spanish and French editions also available.*

0920
021

THE ULTIMATE SONGBOOKS

Hal•Leonard® PIANO PLAY-ALONG

These great songbook/audio packs come with our standard arrangements for piano and voice with guitar chord frames plus audio. The audio includes a full performance of each song, as well as a second track without the piano part so you can play "lead" with the band!

HAL•LEONARD®
7777 W. BLUEMOUND RD. P.O. BOX 13819 MILWAUKEE, WI 53213

Order online from your favorite music retailer at
halleonard.com

Prices, contents and availability subject to change without notice.

KEYBOARD STYLE SERIES

THE COMPLETE GUIDE!

These book/audio packs provide focused lessons that contain valuable how-to insight, essential playing tips, and beneficial information for all players. From comping to soloing, comprehensive treatment is given to each subject. The companion audio features many of the examples in the book performed either solo or with a full band.

BEBOP JAZZ PIANO
by John Valerio

This book provides detailed information for bebop and jazz keyboardists on: chords and voicings, harmony and chord progressions, scales and tonality, common melodic figures and patterns, comping, characteristic tunes, the styles of Bud Powell and Thelonious Monk, and more.
00290535 Book/Online Audio $21.99

BEGINNING ROCK KEYBOARD
by Mark Harrison

This comprehensive book/audio package will teach you the basic skills needed to play beginning rock keyboard. From comping to soloing, you'll learn the theory, the tools, and the techniques used by the pros. The accompanying audio demonstrates most of the music examples in the book.
00311922 Book/Online Audio $16.99

BLUES PIANO
by Mark Harrison

With this book/audio pack, you'll learn the theory, the tools, and even the tricks that the pros use to play the blues. Covers: scales and chords; left-hand patterns; walking bass; endings and turnarounds; right-hand techniques; how to solo with blues scales; crossover licks; and more.
00311007 Book/Online Audio $22.99

BOOGIE-WOOGIE PIANO
by Todd Lowry

From learning the basic chord progressions to inventing your own melodic riffs, you'll learn the theory, tools and techniques used by the genre's best practicioners.
00117067 Book/Online Audio $17.99

BRAZILIAN PIANO
by Robert Willey and Alfredo Cardim

Brazilian Piano teaches elements of some of the most appealing Brazilian musical styles: choro, samba, and bossa nova. It starts with rhythmic training to develop the fundamental groove of Brazilian music.
00311469 Book/Online Audio $19.99

CONTEMPORARY JAZZ PIANO
by Mark Harrison

From comping to soloing, you'll learn the theory, the tools, and the techniques used by the pros. The full band tracks on the audio feature the rhythm section on the left channel and the piano on the right channel, so that you can play along with the band.
00311848 Book/Online Audio $19.99

COUNTRY PIANO
by Mark Harrison

Learn the theory, the tools, and the tricks used by the pros to get that authentic country sound. This book/audio pack covers: scales and chords; walkup and walkdown patterns, comping in traditional and modern country, Nashville "fretted piano" techniques and more.
00311052 Book/Online Audio $19.99

GOSPEL PIANO
by Kurt Cowling

Discover the tools you need to play in a variety of authentic gospel styles, through a study of rhythmic devices, grooves, melodic and harmonic techniques, and formal design. The accompanying audio features over 90 tracks, including piano examples as well as the full gospel band.
00311327 Book/Online Adio $19.99

INTRO TO JAZZ PIANO
by Mark Harrison

From comping to soloing, you'll learn the theory, the tools, and the techniques used by the pros. The accompanying audio demonstrates most of the music examples in the book. The full band tracks feature the rhythm section on the left channel and the piano on the right channel, so that you can play along with the band.
00312088 Book/Online Audio $19.99

JAZZ-BLUES PIANO
by Mark Harrison

This comprehensive book will teach you the basic skills needed to play jazz-blues piano. Topics covered include: scales and chords • harmony and voicings • progressions and comping • melodies and soloing • characteristic stylings.
00311243 Book/Online Audio $19.99

JAZZ-ROCK KEYBOARD
by T. Lavitz

Learn what goes into mixing the power and drive of rock music with the artistic elements of jazz improvisation in this comprehensive book and CD package. This instructional tool delves into scales and modes, and how they can be used with various chord progressions to develop the best in soloing chops.
00290536 Book/CD Pack............................$17.95

LATIN JAZZ PIANO
by John Valerio

This book is divided into three sections. The first covers Afro-Cuban (Afro-Caribbean) jazz, the second section deals with Brazilian influenced jazz – Bossa Nova and Samba, and the third contains lead sheets of the tunes and instructions for the play-along audio.
00311345 Book/Online Audio $19.99

MODERN POP KEYBOARD
by Mark Harrison

From chordal comping to arpeggios and ostinatos, from grand piano to synth pads, you'll learn the theory, the tools, and the techniques used by the pros. The online audio demonstrates most of the music examples in the book.
00146596 Book/Online Audio $19.99

NEW AGE PIANO
by Todd Lowry

From melodic development to chord progressions to left-hand accompaniment patterns, you'll learn the theory, the tools and the techniques used by the pros. The accompanying 96-track CD demonstrates most of the music examples in the book.
00117322 Book/CD Pack............................$16.99

POST-BOP JAZZ PIANO
by John Valerio

This book/audio pack will teach you the basic skills needed to play post-bop jazz piano. Learn the theory, the tools, and the tricks used by the pros to play in the style of Bill Evans, Thelonious Monk, Herbie Hancock, McCoy Tyner, Chick Corea and others. Topics include: chord voicings, scales and tonality, modality, and more.
00311005 Book/Online Audio $19.99

PROGRESSIVE ROCK KEYBOARD
by Dan Maske

You'll learn how soloing techniques, form, rhythmic and metrical devices, harmony, and counterpoint all come together to make this style of rock the unique and exciting genre it is.
00311307 Book/Online Audio $19.99

R&B KEYBOARD
by Mark Harrison

From soul to funk to disco to pop, you'll learn the theory, the tools, and the tricks used by the pros with this book/audio pack. Topics covered include: scales and chords, harmony and voicings, progressions and comping, rhythmic concepts, characteristic stylings, the development of R&B, and more! Includes seven songs.
00310881 Book/Online Audio $22.99

ROCK KEYBOARD
by Scott Miller

Learn to comp or solo in any of your favorite rock styles. Listen to the audio to hear your parts fit in with the total groove of the band. Includes 99 tracks! Covers: classic rock, pop/rock, blues rock, Southern rock, hard rock, progressive rock, alternative rock and heavy metal.
00310823 Book/Online Audio $17.99

ROCK 'N' ROLL PIANO
by Andy Vinter

Take your place alongside Fats Domino, Jerry Lee Lewis, Little Richard, and other legendary players of the '50s and '60s! This book/audio pack covers: left-hand patterns; basic rock 'n' roll progressions; right-hand techniques; straight eighths vs. swing eighths; glisses, crushed notes, rolls, note clusters and more. Includes six complete tunes.
00310912 Book/Online Audio $19.99

SALSA PIANO
by Hector Martignon

From traditional Cuban music to the more modern Puerto Rican and New York styles, you'll learn the all-important rhythmic patterns of salsa and how to apply them to the piano. The book provides historical, geographical and cultural background info, and the 50+-tracks includes piano examples and a full salsa band percussion section.
00311049 Book/Online Audio $19.99

SMOOTH JAZZ PIANO
by Mark Harrison

Learn the skills you need to play smooth jazz piano – the theory, the tools, and the tricks used by the pros. Topics covered include: scales and chords; harmony and voicings; progressions and comping; rhythmic concepts; melodies and soloing; characteristic stylings; discussions on jazz evolution.
00311095 Book/Online Audio $19.99

STRIDE & SWING PIANO
by John Valerio

Learn the styles of the stride and swing piano masters, such as Scott Joplin, Jimmy Yancey, Pete Johnson, Jelly Roll Morton, James P. Johnson, Fats Waller, Teddy Wilson, and Art Tatum. This book/audio pack covers classic ragtime, early blues and boogie woogie, New Orleans jazz and more. Includes 14 songs.
00310882 Book/Online Audio $22.99

WORSHIP PIANO
by Bob Kauflin

From chord inversions to color tones, from rhythmic patterns to the Nashville Numbering System, you'll learn the tools and techniques needed to play piano or keyboard in a modern worship setting.
00311425 Book/Online Audio $19.99

HAL•LEONARD®

Prices, contents, and availability
subject to change without notice.

www.halleonard.com